Cash Flow Statement Basics

From Confusion to Comfort in Under 35 Pages

I0472685

By Axel Tracy

Disclaimer

The material in this publication (the "book") and the information accessed through it is of a general nature only and does not contain investment recommendations or professional advice. The information is not to be relied upon as being accurate, complete or up to date. Axel Tracy (the "author") recommends that, before acting or not acting upon information contained or referred to in this book, readers should seek independent professional advice that takes into account their financial situation, investment objectives, particular needs and/or other personal circumstances. The information contained in this book is not to be used for any purpose other than educational purposes and it is not to be construed as an indication or prediction of future results from any investment. Axel Tracy does not offer financial, business or academic advice. To the maximum extent permitted by law, the author and publisher disclaim all responsibility and liability to any person, arising from directly or indirectly from any person taking or not taking action based upon the information in this publication.

For Sarah: Here's to the next ten years.

For My Grandparents: Thanks for the lessons, the love and always being able to turn to you in need.

Table of Contents

About the Author

Axel Tracy is an accounting and business student at the University of Technology, Sydney (UTS) and is a new financial planning student at the Northern Sydney Institute. He has a passion for his studies and is a member of the invitation-only Golden Key International Honours Society in recognition of having a GPA that placed him in the top bracket of students at his university. He is also a member of the UTS Honour Society.

He was employed by the University of Technology, Sydney, to run PASS sessions in the subject of Accounting Standards and Regulations, an undergraduate accounting subject that trains students to become familiar with Australia's implementation of International Financial Reporting Standards, the current Australian accounting standards regime. He was also employed by UTS as a one-on-one tutor for the study of another 2nd year accounting subject, Accounting for Business Combinations, a subject that dealt with the financial accounting of corporate groups, joint ventures and associates.

Since April, 2011, he has been the Founder & Manager of RatioAnalysis.net, a website dedicated to financial and accounting ratios.

In August, 2013, Axel launched accofina.com. This website promotes the sale of products involved with accounting and finance knowledge and education.

Axel lives in Armidale, Australia, and apart from studies or working on accofina, enjoys spending time with his partner, Sarah, relishing a good cup of coffee or indulging in too much CNBC.

Axel's 'Amazon Author' Page: **amazon.com/author/axeltracy**

About accofina.com

accofina.com launched in August, 2013, and is a hub for accounting & finance knowledge and technology.

On the website you will find Books (Free & Paid), iOS Apple Apps, Online
Courses & Tutorials, Free MS Excel Spreadsheets and other Free Online
Calculators all customized to assist putting academic accounting & finance knowledge, through technology, in the hands of businesspeople, investors and students.

accofina.com is part of Bidi Capital Pty Ltd, which is a company founded, directed and owned by this book's author, Axel Tracy.

Introduction

Welcome to the final instalment of the Financial Statement Basics series: Cash Flow Statement Basics.

The cash flow statement is probably the most underestimated (and often most ignored) of the three main financial statements. Yet its power to outline the status of a business is truly astonishing! It can tell you the stage of the business within its lifecycle or the strategy taken by management or even the success (and viability) of a business as a going concern.

Within this brief book, you will learn how to extract all this information (and more) from any cash flow statement you come across.

There are a few changes in this instalment that will be outlined soon, but you will find that Cash Flow Statement Basics follows a similar path to Balance Sheet Basics and Income Statement Basics with the same conversational tone and once again looking at the real-world financial statements of Amazon Inc.

So what exactly is this book about? It's about learning how to navigate and understand the cash flow statement. The cash flow statement, along with the income statement and the balance sheet, are the three main financial statements produced by a financial accounting system. The financial statements are concise, accounting theory driven summaries of a business and its activities over a period of time or at a particular point in time.

Financial statements are used by both those outside and inside the business to get a birds-eye view of all the financial activity of a business. Within this financial activity you can trace a story about what is going on inside the business, and if you can do this 'story-telling' well then you, as an investor or manager, can make intelligent decisions about how to move forward with your investment and business decisions.

Each of the three main financial statements serves a different purpose in telling the story. The balance sheet, through its assets, liabilities and equity, allow you see through one window. The income statement, with its revenue, expenses and profit, let you look through another window and see a different angle. The cash flow statement offers yet another view and its purpose is to trace the cash in the business: where it came from and where it left. This is done through the classification of operating, investing and financing cash flows.

Like I have said in previous books, while the study of accounting can take a lifetime to master, the fundamentals are not too difficult to grasp. And even a basic understanding of accounting will often dramatically change how you approach your business or investments. It will also put you in a very select group; my accounting lecturers often remind us that there is an extreme lack of accounting literacy in the business world. Thus just a short investment in accounting education will immediately ramp you up to an upper percentile.
I wish you the best over the coming pages and offer my thanks for giving this book the time that you are now.

Naming Conventions

As in previous titles, I would like to give notice that the financial statements often have various naming conventions. Thankfully, the cash flow statement naming conventions are nothing like the balance sheet or (worse yet) the income statement.

The main alternative name for the cash flow statement is 'the statement of cash flows' or in a large corporate group, 'consolidated statement of cash flows' (because the financial statements have been consolidated within a group of companies). You may also see it referred to (or really shortened to) simply as 'cash flow', as it's titled in Google Finance.

Formatting

I am writing this book from Australia, while looking at the cash flow statement of a US listed company from an financial data website. Thus, almost all these factors become variables when it comes to how I am presented with the actual statement. I.e. business location, business size or structure, source of the statement or even finance department preference all result in particular cash flow statement formatting. In fact, the IASB (the international accounting rule setters) and resulting IFRS rules allow the particular presentation of the statement to be based on individual business appropriateness, rather than a dogmatic structure.

But all these differences are superficial and particular peculiarities within these variables can simply be seen as different accents within the same language. That is, if you went to the UK (from the US) the locals would sound different but they are still speaking English. Your initial interaction with the dialect may be a little confusing, but it wouldn't stop you conversing, and soon enough the accent would be imperceptible. So yes, you will come across various formatting conventions of the cash flow statement, but they are all using the same accounting language and they are all saying the same thing.

So if you are brand new to accounting: don't stress! Treat any new format something like a new website you're browsing: scan the statement quickly from top to bottom, bottom to top, look for headings and emphasised text and even look at the numbers and try and find any logic in the arithmetic. I'm sure you'll be 100% fine, in fact it's really not that confusing at all; I'm even thinking this section is a bit of overkill (as I write it) considering how much time I've spent discussing it.

What's Different from Previous Titles in this Series?

While the second title in this series (Income Statement Basics) was very similar in structure to the initial title (Balance Sheet Basics), in this third and final title I wanted to make some major changes in the structure. Thus I thought it would be best to include this section near the start of the book to both acknowledge the shift in structure and that there is a lack consistency in this final title from the first two. I wanted to 'warn' readers of the previous titles that there will be some changes and to explain my reasoning behind this.

Increased use of Sub-Headings and Sub-Sections

Let's start the changes immediately, ha! You will find that this title will be less long prose and more bite-size lessons. I wanted to make it less like a 'novel' that is read like a story from beginning to end and more like a tutorial where you can jump back and forth from section to section and highlight or take notes with easily-identifiable references to where the notes were sourced from.

Working from Example Statement Bottom-to-Top and not Top-to-Bottom

In the earlier titles I referred to real-world Amazon Inc. financial statement and worked through it, line by line, from top to bottom. In Cash Flow Statement Basics I will be working through the statement in reverse: from bottom to top.

I have done this for two reasons. First, the more complex section rests at the top, in terms of the different formatting of the cash flow statement. Thus, I would like to work you into it slowly before blasting you with the hardest part first.

Secondly, the life cycle of a business normally begins with activity in the bottom section of the cash flow statement. Thus, it seems more logical, in a real-world chronology, to begin at the bottom of the statement.

Section Structures Repeat Throughout

I will explain my reasoning for this change before explaining this change directly. My most successful book has been Ratio Analysis Fundamentals. This title (which is outside this particular series) has far outsold any book I have written to date. This apparent success is something I cannot explain definitively even to this day. It's surprising, as I would have thought that books on financial statements would have much broader appeal than the more niche topic of ratio analysis. The biggest suspicion I have as to why readers have preferred

Ratio Analysis Fundamentals, and my hypothesis from here, is that the book is very much structured as a tutorial that has a set format and repeating structure throughout, with only particular ratios and respective content changing through the book. Thus, I will by trying to replicate this repeating, course-like structure.

So, you will quickly see in this book that each section of this book is rather similar to the last. Only the particular section of the cash flow statement and the respective section content will change. This change feeds into the earlier 'Sub-Heading and Sub-Section' change; I would like this book to be more like a brief readable course with actionable lessons throughout.

Accounting (for many) is hardly the most thrilling topic to read about, so I would like this book to be more tutorial-like where readers can apply learned skills after reading particular content.

More Analysis Sections and Less Accounting Theory

The previous two books followed a structure where the example financial statement was explained line-by-line with accompanying lessons on particular accounting theory that led to that particular line item or account.

Cash Flow Statement basics discusses less of this accounting theory (behind each line item) and focuses more on conducting analysis that may be behind some of the cash flow statement results.

While this is only on 'basics' book and thus cannot conduct a comprehensive guide to analysis for every possible outcome, I'm hoping this new focus may be more practical for you and other readers rather than being too theoretical in nature.

The Cash Flow Statement in a Few Paragraphs

Before we spend the remainder of the book diving into the cash flow statement, I would like to very briefly explain the statement in only a few paragraphs. Ideally this will give you a guide into where we are going and also provide quick primer as we approach each section.

So what is the cash flow statement? Simply, it tells us about cash inflows and outflows of a business over a length of time.

Further, it categorises cash flows into particular business activities that give the statement reader further insight into the status of the business, whether it's performing successfully, whether it's expanding or winding down or whether it's raising cash among other things.

A standard cash flow statement will show a net change in cash over the period. It may only show this net change or it may show a cash starting balance, an ending balance and thus also the resulting net change.

This net change in cash is also broken down into three main (and standard) categories. These are cash flow from operating activities, cash flow from investing activities and cash flow from financing activities.

Cash Flow from Financing Activities

From latter to first: cash flow from financing activities displays all cash inflows and outflows that have to do with how the business is financed. That is, how it raises cash from external parties to fund the business (inflows) and how it then returns cash to those who funded the business (outflows).

Cash Flow from Investing Activities

In the second section, cash flow from investing activities, details of all cash inflows and outflows are outlined in respect to investments and sales of non-current assets. These are the long-term assets of the business that normally generate the income of the business.

Cash Flow from Operating Activities

This section of the cash flow statement details the nuts and bolts of the business. That is, this section outlines cash inflows and outflows of the day-to-day operations of the business. For example, if the statement is for a bookstore, then the cash flow from operations would detail money coming in and out in the process of actually selling books. You could contrast this with selling shares to raise the cash to open a bookstore (cash flow from financing activities) and spending funds on buying a retail space to sell books (cash flow from investing activities).

Cash Flow Equation

While there is no formal detail of a cash flow equation in the statement, I thought it might be handy to outline how you calculate the net change in cash given in the statement. It is simply:

Cash at Beginning of Period

+ Cash Flow from Financing Activities

+ *Cash Flow from Investing Activities*

+ *Cash Flow from Operating Activities*

= *Cash at End of Period*

And thus 'Net Change in Cash' is simply:

Cash at End of Period – Cash at Beginning of Period

Well, that's all there is to it! Where the beauty lies is being able to dissect these sections and gauge the performance, position and lifecycle of the business. And that is what we'll be learning how to do over the following pages. Let's get to it!

Example Cash Flow Statements

It's best to take a look at some example cash flow statements upfront so we know exactly what we are referring to throughout. These are below, but please take on board the next few paragraphs (above the examples) so you have a quick explanation of their source, their similarities and where & why they are different.

Why we are using Two Examples

When it comes to cash flow statements there are two different ways to format the cash flow from operating activities. These two different methods result in the 'direct' cash flow statement and the 'indirect' cash flow statement.

We will leave the deep dive into the differences in these formats till later in this book, as I would like to spend some time explaining the two formats and thus it wouldn't be suitable to go into it right now before we reach the heart of the book.

But the key idea here is that instead of using one example with one format or another, we will be showing two examples here, a direct cash flow statement and an indirect cash flow statement.

Similarities & Differences between the Two Examples

As it was just explained, the direct and indirect cash flow statements present the cash flow from operating activities differently. However, when it comes to presenting the cash flow from financing activities and the cash flow from investing activities there is no difference at all. Specifically, the data and presentation is identical.

It is only the operating activities section that has differences and results in the different statement types.

So when you take a look at the examples you will see the financing and investing sections have literally been 'cut and pasted' between the two examples.

There are also two other small differences between the two examples that must be mentioned.

These differences aren't in the nuts and bolts of the cash flow statements but are instead in the accompanying 'supplemental info' that appears at the bottom of each of the two statements.

You will see that the 'cash paid for interest' and 'cash paid for income tax' that appear in the supplemental info of the indirect statement do not appear in the same place as in the direct statement. Within the direct statement these sections (interest & income tax) appear in the operating activities section.

Now, without getting too confusing too early, this particular difference (with tax & interest) is not a specific difference between direct and indirect statements, in general. Rather, where tax and interest appear often comes down to how a particular company chooses to account for these transactions in their particular statements. In other words, you will find this particular difference is company (or transaction) specific rather than being specific to direct and indirect cash flow statements.

If you want to know the exact rules: taxes should appear in operating activities UNLESS the tax cash flows generated are specifically traceable/identified to cash flows that involves financing or investing activities.

As for interest, interest is based on borrowing and lending, which are financing activities, but you will find that the rules that dictate whether something forms part of operating activities cash flows is dependent on whether it is based on "events that enter into the determination of profit or loss", and interest paid and received does in fact help determine profit or loss (and is thus part of operating activities).

Now I will later explain why Amazon Inc. (the source of the indirect cash flow statement example) used supplemental info for taxes and interest, but I thought it would be better to use these line items in, their more usual, operating activities in the direct cash flow statement example (that I generated myself). Just note the conjecture, vague rules & various treatments when it comes to taxes & interest …and hence the final differences between the two example statements.

Source of Examples

Example 1 (Indirect Cash Flow Statement)

As in the previous two titles of this series we will be looking at real-world financial statements. And once again these will be sourced from Amazon Inc. We will be looking at the annual cash flow statements from 2013, that is, from 1st January 2013 to 31st December 2013.

You can find cash flow statements like these from Google Finance or from any listed entity's Investor Relations website.

Below, we will be using the 'Consolidated Statement of Cash

Flows' from Amazon's 2013 Annual Report that I found at the Amazon.com Investor Relations website. The reason for using this version is that it has more detail than the Google Finance option.

Example 2 (Direct Cash Flow Statement)

Because the Amazon Annual Report uses the indirect method for its cash flow statement, I am unable to source a real-world direct cash flow statement for the company. And after a little searching, I found it quite hard to find a listed entity that presents its cash flow statement (in their annual reports) in the direct method.

Due to this apparent lack of availability, Example 2 will NOT be a real-world cash flow statement.

While I will cut and paste the financing and investing sections (as mentioned earlier), I will be creating a 100% fictional operating activities section. So, please, never rely on this example as being a representation of any actual, real business.

Yes, I will be making up the figures so the cash flow equation holds and that everything looks semi-realistic, but this example is for illustration only and shouldn't be relied upon.

What's more important with this example is that you see some of the common operating activity categories that will appear and that you will be able recognise these when you come across them.

Further, it's important that you should be able to differentiate between the direct and indirect cash flow statements and not be thrown a curveball whenever you come across either.

The Cash Flow Statements

Example 1 (Indirect): Amazon, Inc.

	2013
CASH AND CASH EQUIVALENTS, BEGINNING OF PERIOD	
8,084	

Operating Activities

Net Income (loss)	274
Adjustments to reconcile net income (loss)	
to net cash from operating activities:	
Depreciation of property and equipment, including internal-use software and website development, and other amortization	3,253
Stock-based compensation	1,134
Other operating expense (income), net	114
Losses (gains) on sales of marketable securities	1
Other expenses (income), net	166
Deferred income taxes	(156)
Excess tax benefits from stock-based compensation	(78)
Changes in operating assets and liabilities	
Inventories	(1,410)
Accounts receivable, net and other	(846)
Accounts payable	1,888
Accrued expenses and other	736
Additions to unearned revenue	2,691
Amortizations of previously unearned revenue	(2,292)
Net cash provided by (used in) operating activities	5,475

Investing Activities

Purchases of property and equipment, including internal-use software and website development	(3,444)
Acquisitions, net of cash acquired, and other	(312)
Sales of marketable securities and other investments	2,306
Purchases of marketable securities and other investments	(2,826)
Net cash provided by (used in) investing activities	(4,276)

Financing Activities

Excess tax benefits from stock-based compensation	78
Common stock repurchased	0
Proceeds from long-term debt and other	394
Repayments of long-term debt, capital lease, and finance lease obligations	(1,011)
Net cash provided by (used in) financing activities	(539)
Foreign-currency effect on cash and cash equivalents	(86)
Net increase (decrease) in cash and cash equivalents	574

CASH AND CASH EQUIVALENTS, END OF PERIOD

	8,658

SUPPLEMENTAL CASH FLOW INFORMATION

Cash paid for interest on long-term debt	97
Cash paid for income taxes (net of refunds)	169
Property and equipment acquired under capital leases	1,867
Property and equipment acquired under build-to-suit leases	877

Example 2 (Direct): Fictional Biz, Inc.

**CASH AND CASH EQUIVALENTS,
BEGINNING OF PERIOD**
   8,084

Operating Activities

Cash receipts from customers	15,175
Cash payments to suppliers	(2,650)
Cash payments to and on behalf of employees	(6,190)
Interest received (paid)	375
Dividends received	650
Cash refunds (payments) of income taxes	(1,885)
Net cash provided by (used in) operating activities	5,475

Investing Activities

Purchases of property and equipment, including internal-use software and website development	(3,444)
Acquisitions, net of cash acquired, and other	(312)
Sales of marketable securities and other investments	2,306
Purchases of marketable securities and other investments	(2,826)
Net cash provided by (used in) investing activities	(4,276)

Financing Activities

Excess tax benefits from stock-based compensation	78
Common stock repurchased	0
Proceeds from long-term debt and other	394
Repayments of long-term debt, capital lease,	

and finance lease obligations (1,011)

Net cash provided by (used in) financing activities (539)

Foreign-currency effect on cash and cash equivalents (86)

Net increase (decrease) in cash and cash equivalents 574

**CASH AND CASH EQUIVALENTS,
END OF PERIOD** 8,658

SUPPLEMENTAL CASH FLOW INFORMATION

Property and equipment acquired
under capital leases 1,867
Property and equipment acquired
under build-to-suit leases 877

Cash (Flow Statement) is King: The benefits of the cash flow statement.

The cash flow statement is probably the most underestimated financial statement of the three majors. When the income statement determines the "bottom line" and it is the balance sheet that determines the equity and net worth of a business, the cash flow statement is far too often overlooked as a real source of accounting information value. But this is definitely not the case! The cash flow statement offers the reader the third angle into the success and position of a business over a period of time. It offers an insight that the income statement and balance sheet are incapable of showing.

And best of all, it complements the other two statements by sort of mixing the strong elements of both the income statement and balance sheet: you can test the performance of a business (like the income statement) by measuring the changes in net assets and cash over a period. You can test the liquidity & solvency (like the balance sheet) of a business by being able to assess its cash generating ability. And these same tests of cash generation abilities (and how the cash is spent) offer a unique measure on how well a company can adapt to future changes in circumstances and taking advantage of new opportunities.

The starkest benefits, as opposed to reading the income statement or balance sheet for value, will now be broken into the following four generalised sub-sections:

You Spend Cash, not Profits

While financial accounting information is based on specific measurement rules, actual business and economic activity (and all the benefits from these) is based on the concept of earning and spending cash. That is, cash and not profit, is what is ultimately earned, spent & enjoyed by business and society.

Being able to assess how well a business can generate cash, which is what the cash flow statement can do, can guide us on how well a company can adapt to the future. Since business activity requires cash to be spent, having good cash generation abilities can dictate whether a business can take advantage of new opportunities (by changing activities through expenditure) when circumstances change.

On a more negative note, it is not a lack of profits that sends a company out of business, it is instead a lack of cash to meet its financial obligations. Thus, being able to measure changes in the levels of cash and being able to assess cash generation abilities going forward is a key cash flow statement benefit.

Speaking as an investor in a particular business (and with outside investors being a primary user group of financial accounting information), it's important to note that dividends (equity investors) and interest (debt investors) are paid in cash, and cash alone. Therefore the cash flow statement benefits investors through helping determine whether dividends and interest will continue to be paid.

Cash & Different Accounting Methods

As was mentioned just before, there are rules that determine how financial accounting data is measured. However these rules do include flexibility and therefore between two different businesses the same exact transaction can be recorded in the income statement and balance sheet in two different ways. This is one of the negative effects of accrual accounting. The cash flow statement removes accrual accounting by only recognising cash transactions and thus the anomalies of different accounting treatments of the same transaction are removed.

The removal of accrual accounting within the cash flow statement has another benefit. It's commonly known that cash transactions are much harder to deliberately manipulate in financial statements if the business' management was doing something fishy. When companies do deliberately manipulate their accounting results, it is normally done with non-cash accounting transactions.

Finally, the removal of accrual and non-cash transactions in the cash flow statement can show the relationship between cash level changes and accounting profit (in the income statement), with all the unique insights and benefits this entails.

Cash & Valuation

You will often find that many financial analysts and experts base their complex valuation models on some sort of 'net present value' of all the expected future cash flows. This reliance on cash flow data for valuation models means that the cash flow statement is perfect to assist in company and project valuation.

Cash & Business Success

The way the cash flow statement is broken down between financing, investing and operating cash flows does in fact create a unique view into the business that the income statement and balance sheet can't offer.

Based on the cash flows between these three categories you are able to assess the strategy and lifecycle of any particular business at any point in time. You are able to tell if a company is expanding, contracting and all in between.

And from here you are able to evaluate the success of management decisions. You can see if what they are saying in regards to their strategy is actually matching what is being shown in the cash flow statement.

Further, when management states that the business is 'succeeding' you have immediate reference as to whether this business is a real, cash generating machine or otherwise.

Note: As much as I've talked up the Cash Flow Statement, analysing a business is best done through using all three financial statements. These are the balance sheet, income statement and cash flow statement. If you are interested in learning about the other two statement types not covered in this book, you may be interested in the book 'Financial Statement Basics: From Confusion to Comfort in Under 100 Pages'. This title includes 'Balance Sheet Basics', 'Income Statement Basics' as well the book you're reading now all bundled up into one larger title. Learn more about it at **accofina.com/financial-statement-basics.html**

Cash Flows from Financing Activities

Examples of Cash Flows Arising in This Section

1) Cash proceeds from issuing shares or other equity instruments
2) Cash payments to owners to acquire or redeem the entity's shares
3) Cash proceeds from issuing debentures, loans, notes, bonds, mortgages and other short or long-term borrowings
4) Cash repayments of amounts borrowed; and
5) Cash payments by a lessee for the reduction of the outstanding liability relating to a finance lease.

Source: International Accounting Standard 7, Statement of Cash Flows

"Don't forget to also look at the Example Cash Flow Statements at the beginning of this book"

How This Section Feeds into the Cash Flow Equation

Cash at Beginning of Period

+ Cash Flow from Financing Activities

+ Cash Flow from Investing Activities

+ Cash Flow from Operating Activities

= Cash at End of Period

What Does This Section Describe

In accounting terminology, the cash flows from financing activity show changes in the long-term liability accounts and the owners' equity accounts.

In more general terminology, this section shows how the business obtained financial resources (from equity and debt investors) or how the business returned financial resources to the same groups. In other words, how the business is raising and returning capital.

Further, you can see what type of capital is being utilised, being debt or equity. The absolute amounts within the data and the categories (similar to those listed above or in the Amazon, Inc. example) describe both how much and what type of capital is raised or returned.

According to the international accounting standards, one of the key benefits of this particular section of the statement is that it is useful at predicting the future claims on business cash flow by the providers of the business' capital. After all, it is the financiers of the business (owners or lenders) who generally receive the benefits of success, as their capital (with a return) is given back to those groups.

What Could the Results Be Telling Us About the Business

Caveat:

This caveat will appear in all applicable analysis sections and is a reminder that this book is meant to be a concise beginners book. As a result, I cannot offer a completely comprehensive description of every possible situation that could be occurring in any possible cash flow statement. The best analysis requires independent inquiry, critical thinking and even maybe a team, and this book is simply too brief to describe every analytical situation under the sun.

However, the cash flow statement does offer unique & apparent insights into a business' lifecycle, strategy and commercial health.

Final Note: None of the insights below are mutually exclusive. There could be mix of any and all of the situations described.

Business Lifecycle

Starting-Up:

A business that shows high cash inflows in the financing sections may indicate that the business is very new or young.

Generally, the first activity a business undertakes from its existence is to raise capital that will fund the business in its early stages.

For example, a businessperson may want to start an auto parts manufacturing business and they may approach a bank to get a loan. The loan would show up as a cash inflow in the financing section. The same can be said for a young Silicon Valley entrepreneur when they raise seed capital, however this would normally show us as equity financing and not debt.

Winding-Up:

A business showing high cash outflows may be an indicator that the business is winding up or about to close.

When a business is wound up, the last thing it does is pay out all the remaining cash to the owners or lenders of the business. It returns the capital to the financiers as it no longer needs any cash post its existence.

For example, that same auto parts manufacturing businessperson may want to close the business and move into another unrelated line of work. He or she may cease operations, have funds in he bank already and then liquidate all remaining inventory, equipment and property. The complete sum of cash at the end of this process may then pay off the remainder of their bank loan (financing activity outflow) and then return any remaining cash to the shareholders/owners of the business (a similar outflow, but instead an equity outflow).

Business Strategy

Growth Strategies:

Whether raising funds through debt or equity, one of the primary reasons that a business will use external finance (as a strategic measure) is to accelerate growth and take advantage of market opportunities that may be missed if only internal retained earnings were used.

A business has two choices when it wishes to expand (grow), it can use it's own internally generated funds (based on past performance) or it can raise debt/sell equity. Relying on one's own internal funds limits the rate of expansion to the current (or recently experienced) growth rate.

That is, if a business wants to invest $1m in new equipment then building up a cash balance of $1m (to pay for the equipment) is dependant on the current size and growth of the business …and if the business is currently only generating $100k in cash every year then by implication it would take 10-years to have enough cash for the $1m expansion.

However, if that same business made the strategic decision that it wished to grow and expand much faster (possibly taking advantage of a limited time window of opportunity) then it may wish to seek debt finance or equity investment.

In this example, getting access to the $1m for the new equipment may only take a couple of weeks or months. This situation is far quicker than the earlier mentioned 10-years and this decision would fundamentally change how the business operates and succeeds (or doesn't) over the following periods.

With this theoretical explanation of strategic financing decisions out of the way you may be want to know what these alternative situations would look like in the cash flow statement.

A business that chooses the strategy of primarily relying on it's own internally generated funds would show few cash inflows in the Financing Activities section. Unless the business has a very fast internal growth rate this choice is generally regarded as a having a lower growth trajectory than the alternative.

As for the alternative: a business that chooses a high growth strategy will generally be trying to access as much external cash as possible to fund their expansion. This will show up as high cash inflows in the Financing Activities section.

Commercial Health

Rewarding Financiers & Owners:

When all is said and done, a major reason why businesses exist is to financially reward the owners (common stockholders) & all financiers (debt & equity, including stockholders) of the business. Not many people start a business and become the initial stockholders unless there will eventually be a payoff.

The same can be said with other investors; not many equity investors will fund a business unless they are going to see a return on these funds. And we can never doubt that debt financiers (such as a bank) are after their financial return.

That being said, one could argue that when a business is performing well and succeeding as all those involved had hoped for then surplus funds could be returned to the owners & financiers of the business.

So if you take this on board, when you see large cash outflows in the Financing Activities section of the cash flow statement you may assume that the business is succeeding, that it is stable and that it is generating enough cash on its own that it can now afford to return some of the capital that it had earlier sourced from debt and equity financiers.

These cash outflows may be the payoff from success that all those had hoped for.

Struggling to Generate Cash from Core Operations:

If we view the above outflows as a sign of success, we may view high or continued cash inflows in the Financing Activities section as a sign of weaknesses.

Now this may not always be the case, as we just discussed in the lifecycle and strategy section, but for a business to be consistently successful and future-proof itself it must be able to generate a satisfactory level of cash from the core operations of the business. For example, a café must sell enough coffee (consistently) to be successful in the long-term.

A sign that a particular café (for example) may not be selling enough coffee is that it keeps seeking out external finance to fund its operations, i.e. the coffee sales are not funding the operations and instead it is the new finance.

This situation may be shown as high or continued cash inflows within this section of the cash flow statement.

Cash Flows from Investing Activities

Examples of Cash Flows Arising in This Section

1) Cash payments to acquire property, plant and equipment, intangibles and other long-term assets. These payments include those relating to capitalised development costs and self-constructed property, plant and equipment;

2) Cash receipts from sales of property, plant and equipment, intangibles and other long-term assets;

3) Cash payments to acquire equity or debt instruments of other entities and interests in joint ventures (other than payments for those instruments considered to be cash equivalents or those held for dealing or trading purposes);

4) Cash receipts from sales of equity or debt instruments of other entities and interests in joint ventures (other than receipts for those instruments considered to be cash equivalents and those held for dealing or trading purposes);

5) Cash advances and loans made to other parties (other than advances and loans made by a financial institution);

6) Cash receipts from the repayment of advances and loans made to other parties (other than advances and loans of a financial institution);

7) Cash payments for futures contracts, forward contracts, option contracts and swap contracts except when the contracts are held for dealing or trading purposes, or the payments are classified as financing activities; and

8) Cash receipts from futures contracts, forward contracts, option contracts and swap contracts except when the contracts are held for dealing or trading purposes, or the receipts are classified as financing activities.

Source: International Accounting Standard 7, Statement of Cash Flows

"Don't forget to also look at the Example Cash Flow Statements at the beginning of this book"

How This Section Feeds into the Cash Flow Equation

Cash at Beginning of Period

+ Cash Flow from Financing Activities

+ Cash Flow from Investing Activities

+ Cash Flow from Operating Activities

= Cash at End of Period

What Does This Section Describe

The Investing Activities describe the cash flows involved in the changes to the long-term asset accounts of the business. In more general terminology, the Investing Activities section shows how a business purchased (outflows) cash generating assets for the business or sold (inflows) the same types of assets. In other words, how the business is making or liquidating long-term business investments.

You may be aware that the accounting definition of an asset is a resource controlled by an entity that will lead to future inflows of cash. Thus being able to measure the purchase (or sale) of these cash inflow generating assets is one of the key benefits derived from this section of the cash flow statement.

You can see how a business is deploying its funds in the hope of later earning a higher return on these investments.

Similar to the financing section and as described in the example categories listed above, this section will also describe what type of investment (or disposals) are being made, for example whether these are investments in property, plant & equipment (PPE), purchases of equity instruments in other businesses or even assets being created by making loans. The Investing Section will have all these respective classes listed.

The benefit of this particular section, as described by the international accounting standards, is that it gives the reader of the cash flow statement a broad overview of how the business is making expenditures in the running of the business that will lead to an overall increase in future income and cash flows.

What Could the Results Be Telling Us About the Business

Caveat:

This caveat will appear in all applicable analysis sections and is a reminder that this book is meant to be a concise beginners book. As a result, I cannot offer a completely comprehensive description of every possible situation that could be occurring in any possible cash flow statement. The best analysis requires independent inquiry, critical thinking and even maybe a team, and this book is simply too brief to describe every analytical situation under the sun.

However, the cash flow statement does offer unique & apparent insights into a business' lifecycle, strategy and commercial health.

Final Note: None of the insights below are mutually exclusive. There could be mix of any and all of the situations described.

Business Lifecycle

Initial Setup:

We described earlier that high cash inflows in the financing section were an indicator of a business starting up. Following on from this we can say that high cash outflows within the Investing Section are the next logical step in the initial setup of a new business.

That is, once a business has raised it's startup finance, the next step a business will undertake to get the business up an running is to invest in an initial set of cash generating assets. This would be shown as high cash outflows within this section of the cash flow statement.

For example, an electronics retailer has initially sourced a bank loan as start up capital. These newly sourced funds may then be deployed to purchase a retail site and maybe then delivery trucks. These asset purchases (the retail site and delivery trucks) are requirements in the initial setup of the business (the business can't operate without these) and would be shown as Investing Section outflows.

Liquidation prior to Wind-Up:

At the other end of the business lifecycle and once again linking the ideas described in the financing section, if an Investing Section shows high cash inflows then this may be describing a business that is approaching the end of its life; it may be going through the liquidation stage prior to the final wind-up.

When the management of a particular business has made the certain decision that it wishes to close down and no longer operate then it has the responsibility to remove itself from the commercial landscape and return a final set of funds to the financiers & owners of the business. This would normally involve liquidating all saleable assets, pooling all cash (including from the just mentioned sales) and making a final cash payment to owners and financiers. The process of asset liquidation would be shown within the cash flow statement as high cash inflows in the Investing Section, remembering that this section shows changes in the long-term asset accounts.

For example, that same electronics retailer has now decided to close down. It would now no longer need the retail site or delivery trucks (and would need to return all funds to owners & financiers) and thus it would sell these long-term assets. This would result in high Investing Section inflows.

Business Strategy

Expansion:

A business that shows high cash outflows in the Investing Section can be an indicator that the business is undergoing a period of expansion.

When a business wishes to make the strategic decision to expand and increase the scale of its operations it must invest in assets beyond the normal replenishment of its current asset base. That is, if it wishes to generate income beyond its current level this would require a level of assets (that would generate this higher level of income) greater than what currently stood.

This increased level of assets would be shown as high cash outflows in the Investing Section of the cash flow statement.

The example we can use here is one of a bookkeeping service business that wishes to expand into a new region of the United States. Within its current situation it has a fully equipped commercial office in Seattle and a certain level of property, plant & equipment within the long-term asset accounts would measure this.

But management has made the strategic decision that would

like to expand operations (and hopefully grow future income) by moving into the Los Angeles market. It decides to simply replicate its Seattle operations within a second region and thus decides to make an investment in a second fully equipped commercial office.

As the new commercial office and furnishings are purchased this would be shown as high cash outflows in the Investing Section as the property, plant & equipment account is increased.

Contraction:

The opposite of what we just talked about can be said in regards to a strategic decision to contract a business.

In that case there would be Investing Section cash inflows as assets were sold to reflect the business decreasing in size.

We won't focus on this situation beyond we was just said (as the explanation is just the reverse of the mentioned expansion section).

Transition in Operations:

A more unique situation that could be indicated within this section is when a business is transitioning its operations. This particular situation may occur when a business has altered it's strategy as is changing the nature of its business, for example changing its geographic footprint of maybe the lines of business it operates within.

If this is the case then certain assets (that were part of the old way of the business was run) may be liquidated, and thus be shown as high cash inflows, and new assets (that will form part of the new way of doing business) may be purchased and thus be shown as high cash outflows.

Depending on how quickly this transition takes place will determine the timeline between when these inflows and outflows take place in a cash flow statement or number of cash flow statements.

Commercial Health

Expansion as a Result of Success:

As was earlier discussed, high cash outflows can be an indicator of business expansion as an entity purchases more and more long-term assets. If we link this idea with the theory that most businesses want (at their very core) to grow and expand consistently over time then we may be able to draw a conclusion that when a business is expanding then it is showing signs of overall success, and strong commercial health, with its core operations.

That is, if a business is achieving its overall objectives, performing well and selling all the widgets it planned to, then it may be generating enough cash to comfortably fund an expansion and increase the scale of its widget sales operation.

This situation of strong commercial health may be indicated by continued cash outflows in the statement.

Liquidations to Cover Weak Operations:

The situation may be the reverse when there are continued inflows within the Investing Section. This situation may be an indicator of weak commercial health.

When it comes down to it, a business would like to be generating its cash from the core operations. Ideally, selling widgets at a profit should be generating enough cash to fund all the activities and actions of the business. Thus, it may be a sign of weakness if a business is relying on liquidating assets (Investing Section cash inflows) to fund its activities.

A business may be in need of quick cash, perhaps to pay off debt or otherwise continue core operating activities, and the only source of funds may be to liquidate assets.

While there is nothing specifically impractical about this strategy, it can definitely be seen as only a short-term strategy and could even be very disruptive to future plans.

It is short-term in nature as there are only so many assets you can sell; you can't sell assets forever! And it may be disruptive to future plans as it is the long-term assets that generate future income and if you start 'selling the farm' then a business will be less capable of generating income down the track.

Cash Flows from Operating Activities

Why This Section Has Been Left Till Last

When it comes to cash flow from Operating Activities many regard this at the most important section of the cash flow statement. You may then be wondering why it has been left till last, within this book, of the three main sections.

There are two major reasons why this has been done so:

(1) To account for the chronology of a standard business and how this fits into the business lifecycle that has been described.

(2) The fact that the cash flow from Operating Activities can be presented in two separate, but two equally valid, formats. These two formats create the 'direct' and 'indirect' cash flow statements.

While the International Accounting Standards Board encourages the use of the direct method, you will find that a vast many companies instead use the indirect method. In fact, within my own local jurisdiction (Australia) the accounting regulators require that a reconciliation of Operating Activities cash flows to net income also be provided within a financial report (which is almost, if not, identical to the indirect method) if the direct method is otherwise chosen.

Being able to understand and navigate both the direct and

indirect methods of Operating Activities cash flows really is a required skill if you wish to tackle cash flow statements on an ongoing basis. While they ultimately report the same information (changes in cash flow from operating activities), their presentation is starkly different, and do indeed contain different component pieces of data within.

To the uninitiated, financial statement rookie the 'complication' created by the two different statement formats may have been a little too confusing to introduce earlier in the book. Now that you have covered much of the cash flow statement already and been introduced to complimentary theory, taking on the two different statements is a much easier bridge. Hence, cash flow from Operating Activities has been left till last.

Business Chronology

Have you noticed as you progress through this book, within the financing & investing activities sections, that the business lifecycle has been following some sort of chronology?

First we talked about a start-up raising finance (financing activities) and then we talked about using this capital to make asset investments that will hopefully generate future income (investing activities). Well operating activities is the next step of this process, we now have everything in place (from financing and investing activities) and it's now time to get down to it and run the actual business.

If you can grasp the above paragraph at this point, then you may already have a clear understanding of what cash flow from Operating Activities is describing within its section. The lifecycle flow and implied understanding (just mentioned) of what this cash flow statement section displays is a core reason why this section is left till last in the book.

Direct & Indirect Cash Flow Statements

At the beginning of this chapter and also earlier in the book we discussed that there are two different formats for the Operating Activities cash flows. Beyond this earlier introduction, now we will just get down to explaining what makes up the two formats ...just don't forget the key idea that the same information (underlying cash flows) are being displayed, only how these are presented is different.

Direct Cash Flow Statement:

The direct cash flow statement takes all cash transactions (within the Operating Activities section) and groups them according to major classes, for example 'cash receipts from sales of goods' or 'cash payments to employees'.

You will find that categorising cash transaction according to classes is a very similar formatting option to what is used in (and what you have already read about) the financing and investing cash flow sections. In other words, a direct cash flow statement will look and feel similar between all sections of the cash flow statement.

The International Accounting Standards Board (IASB) encourages businesses to use the direct method on the premise that is better assists the cash flow statement readers in estimating future cash flows, as opposed to the indirect method that may disguise this predictive information.

Indirect Cash Flow Statement:

The indirect method presents the same underlying information but takes a different route to get there. What the indirect method does is take net income as a starting figure and then works backwards, by adjusting net income for non-cash accounting transactions, to reach the final cash flow from operating activities.

This method will thus appear not as a section of 'classes of transactions' but instead as a series of non-cash adjustments, from net income to operating activities cash flows. For instance, 'net income' plus 'depreciation/amortisation', plus or minus 'deferred taxes', plus or minus 'changes in working capital', etc.

This method appears more like an arithmetic process as opposed to the classification process within the direct method.

Examples of Cash Flows Arising in This Section

IMPORTANT NOTE: While the direct and indirect methods look different in presentation, they both capture the same underlying examples of cash flows listed here. That is, the examples listed below are actual Operating Activities cash flows irrespective of how they are presented, direct or indirect.

1) Cash receipts from the sale of goods and the rendering of services;
2) Cash receipts from royalties, fees, commissions and other revenue;
3) Cash payments to suppliers for goods and services;
4) Cash payments to and on behalf of employees;
5) Cash receipts and cash payments of an insurance

entity for premiums and claims, annuities and other policy benefits;

6) Cash payments or refunds of income taxes unless they can be specifically identified with financing and investing activities; and

7) Cash receipts and payments from contracts held for dealing or trading purposes.

Source: International Accounting Standard 7, Statement of Cash Flows

"Don't forget to also look at the Example Cash Flow Statements at the beginning of this book"

How This Section Feeds into the Cash Flow Equation

Cash at Beginning of Period

+ Cash Flow from Financing Activities

+ Cash Flow from Investing Activities

+ Cash Flow from Operating Activities

= Cash at End of Period

What Does This Section Describe

As was implied earlier in the context of the business chronology, the cash flows from Operating Activity provide information on how the cash generates and spends cash in regards to core functions of the business.

If we looked upon Amazon Inc. as an online book retailer (which is a simplification considering the vast array of activities Amazon actually undertakes) then the cash flow from Operating Activities would describe how Amazon spends and makes cash running a book store and selling books, i.e. cash flows from its core *operations* or functions.

The same can be said with any business and any cash flow statement, the Operating Activities are the 'nuts and bolts' of running that particular business. Anything that involves spending or generating cash in the sale of widgets, or whatever, is displayed here.

It was mentioned earlier that many regard the Operating Activities section as the most important section of them all. The emphasis on this section is not misplaced. After all, analysing cash flows within Apple's iPhone selling business or understanding cash flows in The Coca-Cola Company's beverage sales business is critical in justifying the ongoing and very existence of these companies, for example.

Beyond this, even the International Accounting Standard on the Statement of Cash Flows from the IASB (which has been referenced throughout this book) details the important nature of this section.

The Standard describes that the Operating Activities section will give the reader an indication on how well a business can generate cash from it's fundamental operations that will allow it to maintain its ongoing capabilities, repay loans, pay dividends and otherwise make new investments to continue and grow the business without needing new external finance.

Not only does a current cash flow statement display information (the most recent historical Operating Activities performance) but this same information when combined with previous cash flow statements, will also offer the reader useful information in predicting future cash flow generation ability.

Overall, when it comes it Operating Activities cash flows, just remember that these are the cash transactions in managing and *operating* the core business activities.

What Could the Results Be Telling Us About the Business

Caveat:

This caveat will appear in all applicable analysis sections and is a reminder that this book is meant to be a concise beginners book. As a result, I cannot offer a completely comprehensive description of every possible situation that could be occurring in any possible cash flow statement. The best analysis requires independent inquiry, critical thinking and even maybe a team, and this book is simply too brief to describe every analytical situation under the sun.

However, the cash flow statement does offer unique & apparent insights into a business' lifecycle, strategy and commercial health.

Final Note: None of the insights below are mutually exclusive. There could be mix of any and all of the situations described.

Business Lifecycle

Growth Stages while either (or both) Finding Feet or Within Growing Industry:

If you find that a business has increasing levels of Operating Activity cash flows then this may indicate, in regards to the lifecycle, that the business is new and undergoing its initial stages of expansion.

That is, as a new business starts to get its name out into the market, builds its reputation and it progresses through the learning curve of operations you will often find that it can regularly improve on its prior period Operating Activities cash flows. This would result in regular increases in this figure.

Note: this phenomenon doesn't distinguish between positive and negative totals within this section. The key idea is that the total is simply improving over time, irrespective of whether to result leads to overall cash outflows or inflows. In fact, you will often find that the younger the business the more likely that the business will have negative cash flows from Operating Activities. This very young business would just have continually smaller and smaller overall outflows over time.

The second condition mentioned in the sub-heading refers to a growing industry. Within a new or growing industry, you may find that this external environment lifts all boats and leads to increasing cash flows from Operating Activities. By implication, if an industry is growing then you can consider that a business is in the earlier stages of its existence. That is, since the industry is expanding then the businesses would still need to reach and go through the apex of the industry and only then its later stages of decline.

Note: Some industries by their very nature are cyclical and go through repeated peaks and troughs in line with economic conditions or other factors, thus it would be important to investigate this to distinguish between a younger, growing industry (and businesses) indicated by increasing Operating Activities cash flows or simply that a business' results are part of an improvement in a cyclical (but maybe older & declining) industry.

Business Reaches 'Cash-Cow' Status:

A (relatively) stable and high level of Operating Activities cash flows is a strong indicator that the business has reached 'cash-cow' status and has everything in place to make it a continually successful business.

So, as we have progressed through the 'Business Lifecycle' sections of this book we have outlined that a business begins its life by raising funds (within the financing activities section) and then it uses these funds to purchase long-term assets (within the investing activities section) and these assets allow the business to maintain the operating capacity of the business and generate income.

From here, and as we just discussed in the previous sub-section, the young business with everything in place then goes through its initial stages of expansion (increasing Operating Activities cash flows).

Now down the track, after all the effort to reach this point, the business is established with well-oiled operations & the industry is some sort of equilibrium.

At this stage of a business' lifecycle you will often find that the there are consistent and relatively stable levels of cash inflows. This is what is termed a 'cash-cow' business; effectively the business owners/farmers can repeatedly draw cash/milk from the fully developed operations of the business/cow.

Business is past its Peak & in Decline:

Most products, businesses and industries have a finite lifecycle. Whether it's the horse & cart in the early 20th century or the cassette tape of more recent years, many businesses will naturally run into decline. While a shift in strategy and product transformation can reinvent a business many times over, it is no surprise that most businesses today were not around 100 or 200 years ago or vice versa.

When it comes to the business lifecycle and the point in time that represents a business is now in natural decline you will often find that these particular business find it harder and harder to generate cash flow from Operating Activities.

Thus, this may be evident within the cash flow statement by a repeatedly weaker result in Operating Activity cash flows. Yes, there may still be overall cash inflows within this section but the trend over time will be a deteriorating figure.

Business Strategy

Firstly, I can think of very few business strategies that wouldn't be aimed at generating the highest level of cash inflow from Operating Activities. This is, after all, the primary purpose of running a business …generating cash from operations!

But there may be a few cases when the structure of cash flows change:

Recent Expansion with Expectation of Growth:

This situation would only (hopefully) be temporary, but if a business believes that there are strong opportunities that can be taken advantage of with an increased level of scale then it may have indeed increased its size, with all manner of extra expenses, without yet growing into its new size of operations. Cash inflows from Operating Activities may have suddenly dropped, in this scenario, as a result of the new higher level of operating outflows without (yet) a corresponding increase in the inflows.

For example, a smartphone manufacturer may believe that with a new factory & more factory staff that it may be able to reduce it's unit costs, which may then lead to new contracts with leading smartphone brands while also taking advantage of the growing smartphone market. The new factory's operating expenses (electricity, maintenance, salaries, etc.) will be incurred from day zero but the planned new contracts & market growth and resulting customer inflows may not show up for a year or two. Operating Activities outflows would suddenly increase (at day zero) and not yet have the corresponding inflows.

Acquisitions or Divestments:

Whether the relative level of inflows versus outflows changes in this case is dependant on the success of this strategy, but if a business undertakes an acquisition of another business then you will most likely see an increase level of aggregate cash flows. That is the absolute value of these cash flows will increase due to the fact that there is a whole new business within this entity's financial statements.

The reverse is true if a business performs a divestment and sells one of its business units. There is one less entire business within the new cash flow statement.

Change in Business Structure, Organisation or Product Offerings:

If there is a fundamental change in how the core business of an entity will be run then there may temporarily be erratic changes in Operating Activities cash flows.

You'll notice cash flows can indeed become predictable when there is little change in the overall running of a business. But when a business makes a strategic decision to change the way it will operate by perhaps changing the organisational structure, the objectives of the business or maybe the products it offers (that is, the core operations of the business) then these changes will become apparent in the cash flow statement.

Until the changes are complete and the core operations of the business become predictable again then there may be transitional changes in the inflows and outflow of Operating Activities.

Commercial Health

Achieving Business Goals & Performing Well:

If a business can achieve consistently high levels of Operating Activities cash flows then there may be few better indicators that a business is performing well and achieving its overall business goals.

Everything that has been presented in this book, in a way, leads to this argument.

The idea that a business starts up & sets up facilities, chooses & finds the best business strategy and releases products that have strong demand all in the hope that it can become successful in its core business operations.

A brilliant indicator of this 'success' is having strong (and ideally growing) inflows within the Operating Activities section of the cash flow statement. It is a black and white indicator that isn't always available from the income statement and balance sheet, alone.

Beyond this, having strong inflows places any business in the best position for long-term success. After all, if there is any possible change that could impact the business in the future what better way to face it and adjust accordingly by drawing on the 'rivers of gold' that the business' operations are providing.

There is only so many times you can tap banks and investors on the shoulder for more money in the future (financing activities) and there are only so many assets you can sell to raise cash for long-term planning adjustments (from the investing activities section). The cash from operating activities is a far deeper well for future resource planning.

What's more (and as was briefly mentioned earlier in the book), if you do want to repeatedly seek external finance from lenders or equity participants, the best reassurance these financiers can have that they will get their return is that the business is generating consistently strong cash flows from Operating Activities. If you can generate cash consistently then you can pay the financiers interest and dividends consistently.

Not Achieving Business Goals & Performing Poorly:

If you can picture the mirror image of what was just described in the previous section then you will already know where I am going in this section…

If a business has Operating Activities outflows or otherwise deteriorating cash flows then this may mean the business is failing to achieve its business goals and is performing badly.

The financing and investing activities sections are used as a foundation to allow success in the Operating Activities section. If you are weak in the latter section then you can't indefinitely rely on the former sections to prop you up.

In regards to outside the cash flow statement, no amount of accounting 'trickery', past results or appearance of strong balance sheets or income statements can protect a business in the long-term if it can't generate sufficient cash from its core operations.

I don't know what else I can say beyond what has been just said and was mentioned in the mirrored previous section, it is never a good sign when a business has weak or weakening results in the Operating Activities section of the cash flow statement.

Final note: Is a series of poor results the death knell for any business at any point in time? The short answer is no. But it is indeed almost always an indicator that something isn't working out as planned or earlier envisaged AND that eventually something is going to have to change within the business to reverse these weak results.

Specific Accounting Issues that may be presented in Cash Flow Statements.

Okay, we are now at a point where we have covered all the fundamental lessons from a standard cash flow statement.

However, when you step out of this 'basics' book and start looking at your own 'real-world' cash flow statements then you may encounter a few issues that seem a little more confusing or at least just out of place as to what we have covered till this point.

These issues are based around accounting practices, disclosures and how cash flow statements preparers (normally accountants) deal with the application of their standardised rules to the less standardised variety found in every single different organisation globally.

We are now going to cover a few of these common issues and explain what they represent or least the logic that leads to their appearance in many cash flow statements.

FX Translation Issues

There are two issues when it comes to businesses that deal in currencies other than their main currency.

Note: The currency a business uses in its financial statements is termed the 'presentation currency'.

Transactions occurring in a Foreign Currency

Things get a bit messy when business has transactions denominated in a foreign currency. This is because of the fact that for 24-hours a day, 5-days a week exchange rates behind these transactions are bouncing all over the place.

How then do cash flow statements account for these oddities? Take an example business that has 1,000,000 transactions during 2016 in Euros when its presentation currency is the US Dollar. How can we interpret and understand the underlying accounting in the 2016 cash flow statement?

Firstly, the businesses will 'translate' the Euro transactions into their USD presentation currency using an exchange rate so all transactions appear as though they are in USD.

But what EUR/USD exchange rate do we use? We are not allowed to just use the exchange rate that prevails at reporting date.

According to financial accounting rules ideally we want to use the exact exchange rate that corresponds with the exact date the transactions took place. But even if we just used daily exchange rates, that means we would have to apply 365 different exchange rates to the 1,000,000 transactions that occurred over the year (depending on what day each of the transactions occurred).

The allowed solution is that you use a weighted average exchange rate for the whole year and apply that one (weighted average) rate to the whole 1,000,000 transactions.

For example if 900,000 transactions occurred on the 1st January first day of the year) and the remaining 100,000 transactions occurred on the 31st December (last day of the year) then you would find the exchange rates for the 1st January ($0.91) and

31st December ($0.97) and then apply weights of 0.9 (900,000 transactions) and 0.1 (100,000 transactions) to these hypothetical rates to achieve an overall weighted average. Or $0.91 x 0.9 + $0.97 x 0.1 = $0.916

Now all 1,000,000 of the 2016 Euro transactions are translated at a rate $0.916 for the 2016 cash flow statement calculations.

Cash Balances held in a Foreign Currency

Now we look at businesses that have cash balances denominated in a foreign currency.

Firstly, a change in value of these foreign balances due to changes in exchange rates is NOT a cash flow. No cash has left or come into the organisation. Only the value of the foreign balance has changed and only in respect to the presentation currency. So you will never find these types of changes appearing in operating, investing or financing activities sections.

However, we do have to account for these value changes and disclose them in the cash flow statement. Why? Because if we have a change in value of foreign cash balances then somehow we need to reconcile all our cash flow statement data to the beginning and ending cash balances.

For example, ABC Company has USD $1,000 and EUR $1,000 in bank accounts on the 1st January. Thus our beginning cash balance (assuming at $0.90 USD/EUR exchange rate) would be USD $2,111 (1000 + (1000 / 0.9)).

And now we move to 31st December and the USD/EUR exchange rate is now $0.95. Assuming the balances are the same our ending cash balance is $2053 (1000 + (1000 / 0.95)). If we then plug in all our actual cash flows for the year into operating, investing & financing then our cash flow equation (which I have presented a number of times) will not balance. It will be out by $58 ($2,111 - $2053).

Equations not balancing are the nightmare of all accountants!

So what do we do? According to financial accounting rules we need to disclose a separate line item on the cash flow statement that reports this FX value change ($58). By including this new line item we can reconcile beginning to ending cash balances and also make the cash flow equation balance.

Note: this new line item must be separate from the operating, investing and financing sections. That is, it is never fed into one of these sections and will normally sit separately at the bottom of the statement (see the Example Cash Flow Statements towards the beginning of the book).

Significant Non-Cash Disclosures

One of the points behind analysing the investing and financing activities sections of any cash flow statement is that it gives the reader an insight into the asset (investing) and capital (financing) structure of the business.

But this insight can be obscured when 'significant' (large and material) transactions occur in the asset or capital structure when no actual cash changes hand.

For example, take a small to medium business that signs up to a number of leases that will provide the use of assets for the business. A business my get an equipment lease from a bank and receive 150 new notebook computers. No cash may have yet changed hand between the bank and business (the first lease payment may occur in 18-months) or between the business and notebook supplier (the bank may have handed over funds directly to the supplier bypassing the business).

So here we have a dramatic expansion in the business' asset base (the notebooks) that could lead to future income and the business has raised external finance (changed the capital structure) that must be paid back down the track, the finance lease. Yet nothing has appeared in the cash flow statement! It kind of defeats many of the analytical benefits I have been harping on about throughout this book.

There is a solution to this problem, but it may not appear directly within the cash flow statement.

The financial accounting standard setters have made it a requirement that if there are any significant non-cash transactions that would otherwise be presented in the investing or financing sections, then these transactions must be disclosed within the overall, complete financial report. In other words, you will find these transactions specified in the 'Notes to the Financial Statements'.

The Notes to the Financial Statements are the pages of detail that come after the main financial statements within the overall financial report of a business. That is, the main financial statements take up 3 to 5 pages at the beginning of the financial report and then after these statements you will find about 60 pages of 'Notes' that provide more detail into the earlier financial statements, all disclosures as well as outlining all the accounting policies. You will find these 'Significant Non-Cash Disclosures' here in these Notes.

Interest & Dividends

This was spoken about earlier in the book when we were discussing the Example cash flow statements. But now we return to the topics of interest & dividends to discuss what the formal rules are according to the IASB & IFRS.

The bad news:

Even the formal IFRS standards aren't clear as to which section interest and dividends should appear.

You will find that different organisations will place these items in either operating, investing or financing sections. So you will need to keep an eye out for this and be aware when you compare statements from two or more different organisations.

According to the rules, these things are clear:

You keep interest and dividends separate in your reporting, you don't combine them as one line item.

Secondly, once a section of the cash flow statement is chosen then the business needs to remain consistent from period to period. That is, if interest is going to appear in the operating section in 2016 then it shouldn't appear (for example) in the financing section in 2017. The classification should remain consistent over time.

This is what is not clear and where there is no consensus:

Interest (cash flows both ways) & dividends received may be considered an operating activity because these flows feed into the determination of profit & loss (as was mentioned when we discussed this earlier).

Dividends paid (not received) do NOT feed into profit and loss and thus you can't make the same argument about them appearing in the operating section. But on the other hand, some cash flow statement readers may want to determine a business' ability to pay dividends from core operations and then in this case you would put in it the operating activities section.

But interest & dividends (inflows & outflows) may also be a financing activity as they involve cash flows in regards to obtaining external financial resources and it involves the capital structure of a business.

Further, interest & dividends (inflows & outflows) may also even be an investing activity as the cash flows may be tied to the return on investment of particular long-term assets.

Confusing? Yes. And why this section is included in the book.

Just remember that the choice will often be company or transaction specific, interest & dividends will always be presented separately and that once a choice is made then the business should remain consistent from period to period and keep the cash flows in the same section.

Taxes

Okay, now we are up to our final tricky section, I hope you are still hanging in there with me.

When it comes to tax cash flows it is another situation where there is no definitive rule about which section the cash flow should appear in. Whether they appear in operating, investing or financing is transaction or accounting period specific.

The general rule is that tax cash flows should appear in operating activities. This feeds back into the idea that tax is involved in the calculation of profit & loss.

But there is an exception. If a specific tax cash flow can be traced to a specific transaction that appears in the investing or financing sections and the transaction and resulting tax cash flow occur in a comparable accounting period, then you may find this tax cash flow appears in the investing or financing section whichever the case may be.

Further, if a business finds that the tax cash flows are a mishmash of operating, investing & financing flows and placing them in a single section would appear inappropriate then a single separate tax flow figure may be disclosed separately from all sections in a new line item. This is what may be the case with the Example Amazon Inc. statement that appears towards the beginning of this book (and as I mentioned I would refer to later).

Final Thoughts

Well that wraps up the book and also wraps up this Financial Statement Basics series! Thanks for your time and interest.

As for final thoughts on this book, I hope that you can keep it both as a reference for the future while also it being only your first step in your cash flow statement analysis journey.

If you want to learn more theory then almost any accounting textbook you could find will provide a chapter or two on the cash flow statement ...and often in more detail than this concise 35-page book.

Further, if you want to go to the source of financial accounting rules then you could always check out 'International Accounting Standard (IAS) 7: Cash Flow Statements'. The International Accounting Standards Board (IASB) is the organisation that has released IAS 7.

The best way to learn about most fields of interest is to put theory into practice. Thus I hope you go, get out there and get a hold of as many real-world cash flow statements that you can handle. Use the lessons in this book as a basis but be prepared to adjust your knowledge for all the intricacies that you will face.

And don't be frightened when you first venture out and various cash flow statements all look a little different! Don't forget about the differences between direct and indirect statements and keep in mind the slightly odd different accounting treatments of things like interest, tax, etc.

You will soon find out that more cash flow statements you look at the easier the analysis process will become. Very quickly you will be able to tell new stories about businesses (from the cash flow statement) that were previously obscured from you. Very quickly you'll realise that this whole process isn't as difficult as first imagined!

Thanks again for your time with this book, I sincerely hope you got more practical value in return than the investment of time & money in reading & acquiring the title.

Best wishes,
Axel Tracy

Extras

Book Excerpt

The book you just read was one of a series of three titles based around learning about financial statements. The other two titles are *"Balance Sheet Basics: From Confusion to Comfort in Under 30 Pages"* and later *"Income Statement Basics: From Confusion to Comfort in Under 30 Pages"*.

Since *Cash Flow Statement Basics* wrapped up the series, all three titles have been bundled into one more comprehensive and complete book, *"Financial Statement Basics: From Confusion to Comfort in Under 100 Pages"*. You can learn more about this title, and how to access it, at **accofina.com/financial-statement-basics.html**.

However, if you would like a taste of the other titles before inquiring any further then please find below an excerpt from *Income Statement Basics*.

The income statement is also known as the profit & loss statement and details the revenue and expenses, over a period, of a particular business. An outcome of an income statement is determining 'net income' or 'net profit' and this figure is a key financial performance indicator for any organisation with the profit motive.

Please enjoy the except, and maybe check out the individual title *Income Statement Basics: From Confusion to Comfort in Under 30 Pages* at Amazon or use the link above to learn about the complete *Financial Statements Basics* series (in one book) and get a discount on the bundle.

Expenses

"Expenses are decreases in economic benefits during the accounting period in the form of outflows or depletions of assets or incurrences of liabilities that result in decreases in equity, other than those relating to distributions to equity participants."
-   *IASB Conceptual Framework 4.25(b)*

Above is the definition of expenses according to the IASB and again it has links to the balance sheet even though expenses are within the income statement. The quickest way to make sense of this obtuse definition is to look at the similarities between it and the IASB definition of income in the last section. You will see rather quickly that the two definitions are mirrors of each other and the language is almost identical (it's just mirrored language). From this you can conclude that expenses are the opposite of income and essentially represent the opposite effect within the Income Statement, that being they subtract economic benefits (money) during an accounting period.

If again these definitions are not your preferred method of learning, the simplest way to look at it is that expenses are the ongoing costs to run the business during a set accounting period. They are things like office rents and marketing expenses. The things you need to pay for in the ordinary course of business. Using a basic definition again and mirroring the earlier statement, we can say that the 'basic' concept is: *Expenses are the monies you spend or incur while in the ordinary course of selling goods or selling services (keeping in mind the accrual accounting concept).*

Expenses take up most of the remaining Income Statement aside from the calculation results. That is, they lie beneath the income section and roll all the way down to the net income figure (aside from calculation results along the way).

Looking at a real-world example you can see Amazon's expenses (within the included Income Statement) include operating expenses, non-operating expenses and tax expenses (tax provisions to be specific).

Before we go any further, it is time to talk about a number of different formatting options to describe how the expenses are set out in the income statement.

Alternative 1a 'Descriptive Format':

This alternative is just the option that Amazon.com has taken in our example. The descriptive format displays the revenue figure and simply subtracts all expenses to leave a net income figure.

You can see with Amazon.com that they have set out their Income Statement with an 'operating expenses' section that provides most of the detail of their day-to-day operations, which is directly below the revenue figures. Amazon divides their ordinary expenses into certain categories (such as Cost of Sales & Fulfilment) and simply allocates all ordinary expenses into one of these categories.

Note: It is often important to read the Notes to the Financial Statements (the 'fine print') to get further clarification into how the brief (1-page) set of results are calculated and allocated. After doing this with Amazon, I found out that they even break down their depreciation expenses into their respective operating expense categories, such as some depreciation for 'Fulfilment' and some depreciation for 'Technology & content'. Many businesses separate out depreciation and amortization and it was only through reading the fine print (the 'Notes') that I learned that they used this particular accounting policy. Different accounting policies can have very wide implications for financial statement analysis, so the more comfortable you are with getting your head around the basics, the more you should delve into the financial statement Notes to get even more detail.

Okay, getting back to topic, in short: the descriptive format shows revenue minus expenses equals net income.

Alternative 1b 'Functional Format':

The next common format is the functional format income statement. While essentially displaying the same information (all income statements essentially show the same thing), the functional format inserts a 'gross profit' section just below the revenue section. That is, revenue minus 'cost of sales' equals gross profit, and only then the rest of the expenses are listed.

The functional format separates out cost of sales and gross profit from all the other expenses. This format is common in retailing and manufacturing business (as 'cost of sales' play a large influence) while the descriptive format is more common in service businesses (as 'cost of sales' play a smaller role).

Here is a quick aside if you are unsure as to what 'cost of sales' are: Cost of sales, a.k.a. Cost of Goods Sold (COGS) or Cost of Revenue, are those expenses/costs which are incurred to get inventory that will later be resold. Perhaps in a retailing business cost of sales are the prices paid to wholesalers for the goods the retailer sells. Or perhaps in a manufacturing business, cost of sales are the costs/expenses incurred in manufacturing products that will later be resold.

Do you see why cost of sales and gross profit figures are vital indicators (and hence the functional format) for businesses that hold inventory? Costs of Sales are unavoidable (and often large) expenses for some businesses so their measurement and ongoing management are very important. And gross profit figures (Revenue minus Cost of Sales equals Gross Profit) are also very important as they represent the starting point to meet all other expenses and net income.

Below the gross profit section, the descriptive format and functional format are the same. It is only the inserted gross profit section that makes the income statement a functional format statement.

Free (and One Paid) Accounting Resources

Introduction to Financial Accounting: Coursera **(coursera.org/learn/wharton-accounting)** If you want a quick, clear and kind of funny series of video lectures and tasks that can get you up to speed with all the fundamentals of bookkeeping and accounting then you may want to check this Coursera course. It's free, published by the Wharton School and has numerous sessions (including archived sessions). It covers accounting fundamentals told through the story of financial statements and ratio analysis.

Google Finance **(google.com/finance)** Google's finance website is still probably one of the individual investor's best free sources of financial data and information on the web. It contains a world-class stock screener, has financial statement information for more companies than you can poke a stick at as well as strong charting capabilities. Seriously, I'm glad Google makes so much money with AdWords so they can offer cool sites like this one for free (…and create driverless cars!)

Investopedia **(investopedia.com)** Investopedia is one of those handy little websites that continually comes up when I'm doing my own bits of research on the net. It has everything from a comprehensive financial dictionary (hence the 'pedia' title), to the latest financial news, to tutorials & exam prep all while being bundled up in a vast array of financial topics from 'personal finance' to 'financial advisors'. Overall, it's great value for a free resource.

Financial Markets: Coursera **(coursera.org/learn/financial-markets)** This Coursera course is your opportunity to be taught by an Economics Nobel Prize winning professor, the famous Robert Shiller from Yale University. This Coursera version is a condensed version of a Yale course, with all the most important bits of financial institutions, markets, history of financial thought and all in between. The quality of the guest speakers you are offered is testament to this course being of the best in the world that is available in a MOOC.

Accounting [9th Edition]: Horngren, Harrison & Oliver (Paid) (amazon.com/Accounting-9th-Charles-T-Horngren/dp/0132569051/) This link takes you to the Amazon Product Page of a recent edition of the accounting book that I used in my first-year accounting studies at university. At UTS we used this book in two semesters of accounting study for both introductory financial and management accounting. If you can get through this dense book (it's a full blown textbook) then you'll be very proficient with accounting overall. I'm pretty sure the link takes you to the US Edition, as I couldn't find my original Australian edition, so it may have wider localised appeal.

Free accofina.com Resources

'accofina' is the business behind this book and within its website, accofina.com, you will find a number of free resources available for download or for use on-site:

Accounting Introduction PDF mini-book **(accofina.com/accounting-foundations.html)** *"Accounting: Foundation Inputs & Outputs"* is a 15-page PDF mini-book which is available for download. It offers some of the basic accounting theory into the inputs and outputs of a financial accounting system. The outputs are the three main financial statements and the inputs being the theory behind accounting data entry.

Capital Budgeting Spreadsheet **(accofina.com/capital-budgeting-excel.html)** If you wish to assess the value of planned large projects and capital expenditures then you may benefit from capital budgeting tools. You can access a spreadsheet that does a lot of number crunching and provides NPVs, pro forma income statements as well as other information just by inputting some key project data.

Time Value of Money Spreadsheet **(accofina.com/time-value-money-excel.html)** The Time Value of Money is one of the most important concepts in finance. This available spreadsheet calculates some of the primary time value of money concepts such as future values, present values and annuities. All formulae are also provided within.

Ratio Analysis Spreadsheet (**accofina.com/ratio-analysis-excel.html**) You will find 17 of the most common financial ratios have been put into a MS Excel Spreadsheet which both calculates the ratios as well as offering the formulae behind them.

Cash Flow Forecast Spreadsheet (**accofina.com/cash-flow-forecast-excel.html**) The final spreadsheet offered by accofina is a 2-year monthly cash flow forecast to assist in planning and control. It provides a strong overview of 24-months and also calculates running balances, aggregate totals and overdraft interest.

Online Finance Calculators **accofina.com** has 25 on-site finance calculators available for use for free. Some calculators involve the cash flow statement and there are a number of other finance, business and investment calculators. They are simple JavaScript calculators where you simply enter the financial data and the calculator displays the result. A brief guidance explanation is also offered with all calculators.

More Books and Other accofina Products

More Books:

1) Financial Statement Basics
http://accofina.com/financial-statement-basics.html

2) Balance Sheet Basics (Book 1 of Financial Statement Basics)
http://accofina.com/balance-sheet-basics.html

3) Income Statement Basics (Book 2 of Financial Statement Basics)
http://accofina.com/income-statement-basics.html

4) Ratio Analysis Fundamentals
http://accofina.com/ratio-analysis-fundamentals.html

5) 331 Great Quotes for Entrepreneurs
http://accofina.com/331-great-quotes-entrepreneurs.html

6) Corporate Finance Fundamentals
http://accofina.com/corporate-finance-fundamentals.html

Online Courses and Tutorials:

1) Financial Statement Fundamentals (Udemy Course)
http://accofina.com/financial-statement-fundamentals.html

2) Udemy Instructor Page
www.udemy.com/u/axeltracy/

3) YouTube
www.youtube.com/accofina

iOS Apps:

1) Ratio Analysis & Management Accounting Calculators
http://accofina.com/management-accounting-ratio-analysis-app.html

2) Ratio Analysis & Management Accounting Calculators 'Lite'
http://accofina.com/lite-management-accounting-ratio-analysis-app.html

3) Profitable Pricing
http://accofina.com/profitable-pricing-app.html

accofina Contact Details and Review Request

You can contact Axel Tracy at accofina anytime and for any reason at any of these contact points. Tell me if you enjoyed the book, or if you could suggest anything for a 2nd edition.

Email: **axel@accofina.com**

Facebook: **facebook.com/accofinaDotCom**

Twitter: **@accofina**

Google+: **https://plus.google.com/+accofina**

Amazon Review Request:

Also, it would be great to get an Amazon Review from you if you enjoyed, and got value, from this book.

Positive Amazon Reviews are worth their weight gold in the Amazon World and could possibly propel my little business, accofina, beyond its wildest expectations.

If you did get a positive experience from this book, it would be deeply appreciated if you could spare a couple of minutes to Rate the Book (on its Amazon product page) and maybe leave a positive Comment. Thanks again.

www.ingramcontent.com/pod-product-compliance
Lightning Source LLC
Chambersburg PA
CBHW021006180526
45163CB00005B/1913